THE DANCING MASTER

A concise biography of Muhammad Ali

Published in 2007

ISBN 978-0-6151-8455-5

For more information on the life and career of Muhammad Ali, visit our website at **http://www.muhammadali-life.com**

Dedication

This book, *"The Dancing Master: A Concise Biography of Muhammad Ali"*, is dedicated to the life and career of this great champion, humanitarian, and world figure. By its presentation, I hope to offer an inspirational look at a man who inspired so many others by his greatness, inside the ring as well as outside. I only hope to do justice to such a bold and courageous personality as Muhammad Ali was and still is, for he continues to give hope to young and old alike by the brave manner in which he faces his present condition. Many would have given up by now, but Muhammad Ali does what Muhammad Ali has always done -- persevere in the face of adversity. His example still stands as a legendary model of strength and patience in a world filled with challenges, trials, and tribulations. I dedicate this book to a living legend, The Greatest of All Time, **Muhammad Ali.**

Contents

INTRODUCTION 5

PART 1   CASSIUS CLAY - THE BEGINNING 7

PART 2   THE BICYCLE 9

PART 3   THE 1960 OLYMPICS - ROME, ITALY 11

PART 4   TURNING PRO 14

PART 5   THE ROAD TO THE TITLE 18

PART 6   HEAVYWEIGHT CHAMPIONSHIP FIGHT 21

PART 7   REMATCH / ALI-LISTON II 28

PART 8   TITLE DEFENSES 33

PART 9   ERNIE TERRELL - MORE CONTROVERSY 39

PART 10 THE DRAFT AND EXILE OF ALI 42

PART 11 THE RETURN OF MUHAMMAD ALI 47

PART 12 MUHAMMAD ALI VS. OSCAR BONAVENA 49

PART 13 "THE FIGHT" - ALI VS. FRAZIER I 52

PART 14 THE SECOND JOURNEY 57

PART 15 THE SETBACK 59

PART 16 THE "RUMBLE IN THE JUNGLE" 63

PART 17 CHAMP ONCE AGAIN 69

PART 18 "THE THRILLER IN MANILA" 71

PART 19 THE DECLINE 76

PART 20 ALI VS. NORTON III 77

PART 21 THE LOSS OF THE TITLE 79

PART 22 THREE-TIME CHAMPION 81

PART 23 COMEBACKS AND RETIREMENT 83

ALI'S BOXING RECORD AND LIST OF FIGHTS 87

FILMS BY OR ABOUT MUHAMMAD ALI 92

MUHAMMAD ALI IN ISLAM 94

EPILOGUE 102

Introduction

On the following pages you will read a biography of Muhammad Ali which will give an inside look at a great Heavyweight Champion, considered by many to be the greatest fighter of all time. This biography, "The Dancing Master", takes a look at some of the main moments in the life of Muhammad Ali, from his introduction to boxing via a stolen bicycle, to his Olympic triumphs, his rise to the Championship, his personal bouts against the U.S. military, and his epic battles in the ring against some of the other great champions of his era.

While this biography of Muhammad Ali does not cover all of the aspects in his life, it does manage to give an overview of the most important events, including a sometimes detailed account of his most memorable fights which will be discussed for years to come. Writing a Muhammad Ali biography was not only eye-opening and awe-inspiring, but was also a great reminder of how faith and conviction can triumph over ignorance, prejudice and misunderstanding. Anyone else who has written a biography of this world-great sports figure would probably agree that you are not quite the same after recalling the events of his life.

With this, I am quite pleased to present what I believe to be a concise, yet honest and sincere biography of the great Muhammad Ali for your reading enjoyment. I hope that this biography will inspire you, as it has inspired me, to take a closer look at your life, examine your higher principles and always stand up for what you believe to be right. Like so many others, I, too, am grateful to Muhammad Ali for his courage, his insight, and his sincerity and for being an excellent model, for young people and old alike, to emulate in a troubled and turbulent world.

On that note, I present "The Dancing Master: A Concise Biography of Muhammad Ali", dedicated to Ali, the greatest fighter of all time.

Part 1 CASSIUS CLAY - THE BEGINNING

Cassius Marcellus Clay, Jr. was born on January 17, 1942, the son of Cassius, Sr. and Odessa Clay, his proud parents. According to his mother, Cassius' first knockout came when he was just a baby, when he stretched out his little arm, hitting his mother in the mouth, and loosened one of her teeth. He grew up on Grand Avenue in Louisville, Kentucky, which was a racially segregated city like most others in the United States at that time. He and his younger brother, Rudolph Clay, used to run and play on 32nd and Greenwood with their friends and would often run to Chickasaw Park with some of the other neighborhood boys.

His father was a sign painter and was a sometimes difficult parent. It has been said that the boys feared their father at times. But they also loved their father, and he loved them, as well, and always wanted the best for his sons. His mother was a little more of an outgoing, freestyle individual, which brought a gentle balance to the Clay household. It is probably more the personality of Clay's mother which the world would come to see in him - outgoing and friendly, but also strong and confident. And it was this very same confidence which would, after certain events to come in his early life, inspire him to do all the things that eventually led him to become Heavyweight Champion of the World.

Part 2 THE BICYCLE

It was in the year 1954 that Cassius Clay, a 12-year old, rode his new bicycle to a Louisville Home Show. He was with a friend and the two of them enjoyed a day of browsing in the auditorium while his bicycle was parked outside. Unbeknownst to young Clay and his companion, though, was that during the day someone had stolen his bicycle while he was inside. When Clay left the auditorium later, he discovered his bicycle stolen and was devastated. He searched for a police officer to report his bicycle stolen, and was led to a basement gym where a local police officer named Joe Martin taught boxing to young boys. Young Cassius, exhibiting some of his inborn confidence, boldly told Officer Martin, "If I find the guy who stole my bicycle, I'm gonna' give him a good whipping". But Officer Martin told Cassius that if he wanted to do that, he better first learn how to fight. He urged Cassius to join the gym class, and young Clay did just that.

 Cassius Clay never did find his bicycle, but what he did find was that he had a natural talent for the sport of boxing. He worked hard at it, and developed those natural skills. Several weeks after joining Officer Martin's gym, Cassius had, and

won, his first fight - a 3 round decision against a novice named Ronnie O'Keefe - and the birth of the world's greatest fighter had taken place in a small basement gym.

Part 3 THE 1960 OLYMPICS - Rome, Italy

Cassius Clay receives Gold Medal at the 1960 Olympics
Source: Sports Illustrated

Over the next several years, Cassius would go on to amass more than 100 amateur bouts, winning six Kentucky Golden Gloves championships, two National Golden Gloves and two National Amateur Athletic Union (NAAU) titles. With such success, it was only natural that the now 18-year-old fighter would be chosen to represent the United States on the world stage - The Olympics. It was 1960, and the Olympics would be held in Rome, Italy. But how would Cassius travel all the way to Rome from Kentucky? By airplane? Cassius wouldn't hear of it. He was deathly afraid of flying. His anticipated participation in the Rome Olympics was in serious jeopardy because he was more afraid of flying than he was eager to fight in the Olympics. But Joe Martin, who first taught young Clay to fight, convinced him that if he did not go, then his dream of one day becoming Heavyweight Champion may never become a reality - for the Olympics was a stepping stone in that direction. Somehow, on the basis of that kind of argument, along with several hours of convincing, young Cassius Clay mustered up the courage to board the plane to Rome, and the sports world has been the better for it ever since.

In the Olympics, Cassius would win his first three fights against boxers from Belgium, Russia, and Australia with relative ease, being too quick and too smart for his opponents. He was now on the brink of a monumental achievement - a Gold Medal in the Olympics. Standing between him and this award was a very experienced fighter from Poland, and a bronze medal winner in the 1956 Olympics, named Zbigniew Pietrzykowski. This Polish fighter was also a three-time European champion and a "southpaw", or a left-handed-style fighter. Olympic fights are only three rounds, so winning each round is very important. Pietrzykowski's experience and southpaw style confused young Cassius in the first round, so Clay fell behind in the scoring of the fight. He was able to do a bit better in Round 2 to even things up. So Round 3 was all important, for it would decide who would win the Gold Medal.

Cassius Clay used his speed, agility, and natural gifts to outbox the more experienced Pole fighter. After the fight, it was the arm of Cassius that was lifted by the referee, signifying that not only had young Clay won the fight, but the Gold Medal, as well. Cassius Clay had won the Gold Medal for the United States of America and would come home as an Olympic Champion.

Part 4 TURNING PRO

Cassius returned to a hero's welcome in Louisville, Kentucky. The native son had represented his country and his hometown in a most remarkable fashion. Young Cassius, in his soon-to-be trademark style, boldly announced to his home crowd that his next goal was to win the Heavyweight Championship of the world. He was an Olympic Champion, but he was still a Light-Heavyweight, had not even turned pro, nor had he even been signed to a single professional fight, yet this brave young man was beginning to let the world know that it was only a matter of time before he would challenge the boxing world in order to take over the reign as champion. How bold an 18-year-old this kid was! But what the world did not know yet was that this was no ordinary 18-year-old. This was the beginning of Muhammad Ali, the greatest fighter of all time.

An eleven-man local sponsoring group in Louisville was chosen to represent the young boxer and help him begin his career as a professional fighter. And, of course, Clay would need a good, experienced trainer to get his career off to a good start. They chose Archie Moore, a great professional fighter who had amassed the greatest knockout record in the history of boxing up to that time. And Archie Moore had been in over 200 fights, so his experience was unquestionable. However, the relationship between this young, brash fighter and the older, seasoned veteran of the ring would not last long at all. Moore wanted Clay to do his part in sweeping the training camp. Clay complained about this kind of work, as well as differences in training styles and strictness, so he decided to look for another trainer. The person they chose was a brilliant trainer, Angelo Dundee, who would come to love Muhammad Ali and stay with him throughout his entire career.

Clay's first professional bout was against a fighter named Tunney Hunsaker in October of 1960 before a home crowd in Louisville, Kentucky. Clay won the fight in 6 rounds. After his pro debut, he went on to fight several other boxers who were not necessarily household names, establishing a record of 10-0 by February of 1962. At this point, Clay met a fighter named Sonny Banks in New York's Madison Square Garden. In the first round, Banks landed a perfect left hook right on the button and, for the first time as a pro, Clay hit the canvas. A clean knockdown, right on the jaw like this one was, could have finished many a fighter, but as Angelo Dundee would later say, "He (Ali) was out on the way down, but woke up as soon as his backside hit the canvas. When he got up so bright-eyed and bushy-tailed, I knew that night that Muhammad had greatness in him." Clay survived the round and went on to register a 4th round TKO.

After Sonny Banks, Clay had a few more bouts which all ended in KO's. By this time, Clay was well into the routine of predicting the rounds in which the fights would end. Cassius would say, *They all fall in the round I call.* And time and time again, his fights would end in just the round he predicted. Alex Miteff in 6, Willie Besmanoff in 7, Sonny Banks in 4, Don Warner in 4, George Logan in 6, etc., etc. But now it was time for Clay to meet a big-name boxer. His opponent was none other than his former trainer, Archie Moore - "The Old Mongoose" - as he was affectionately known.

Clay had 15 professional fights at this point, while Moore was the veteran of over 200 fights. Many thought that Moore's experience and knockout expertise would be a great challenge to a young, comparatively inexperienced fighter like Clay. But Clay was, as usual, loaded with confidence. He said, *I'll get Moore in four*. And sure enough, just as Clay had predicted, he knocked out Archie Moore in round four.

After another successful knockout in the following year, Clay met a fighter named Doug Jones, again in Madison Square Garden in New York. Clay's prediction: "I'll take out Jones in Round 6." He then went on to revise his prediction to 4 rounds. But from Round 1 onwards, Clay found that he had run into a very rough and challenging opponent who gave him lots of trouble. His 4th round prediction failed. His knockout prediction failed. The Doug Jones fight went the entire 10-round distance. Though the fight was close, it still turned out to be a unanimous decision in favor of Cassius Clay.

Part 5 THE ROAD TO THE TITLE

"Enough is enough," thought young Clay. "I want the Heavyweight Title. I want that *'Big Ugly Bear'* ", as he not-so-affectionately referred to the reigning Heavyweight Champion, Charles "Sonny" Liston. Clay would say, *"He's too ugly to be the Champ. The World Champion should be pretty, like me!"* But Sonny Liston paid little attention to this brash, loud-mouthed kid and claimed that if he were to fight Clay, *"...he was likely to be locked up for murder."* Besides, Liston had an upcoming title defense in the rematch against a much more established fighter, former two-time Heavyweight Champion Floyd Patterson, whom he had knocked out several months earlier in the first round to win the title.

It wasn't Clay's time yet, so he went to England to fight a veteran boxer named Henry Cooper. Cooper did not seem to be a threat to Cassius, so Clay did not take him too seriously. Clay said, *"I'm not trainin' too hard for this bum, Henry Cooper is nothing to me, and if this bum goes over five rounds, I won't return to the United States for 30 days, and that's final!"*

For three rounds, Clay had his way with Cooper, using his superior speed and boxing skills to outclass the gentleman from England. And he continued this trend throughout the fourth round until, with only seconds left in the round, Henry Cooper threw what some referred to as "Henry's Hammer", a powerful left hook which landed flush on Clay's jaw. Clay fell down hard into the ropes just before the bell sounded. He stood up but was clearly dazed and stunned as he was guided over into his corner. Clay was in big trouble. But his quick thinking trainer, the brilliant Angelo Dundee, noticed a slight tear in Clay's boxing glove and proceeded to "help it along a bit" by opening the tear wider and informing the referee that Clay's glove was damaged. In the following minutes, there was a delay in the fight while they looked for a replacement glove. None was found, so Dundee said, *"Never mind, we'll just use what we have."* But by this time, Clay had a chance to clear the cobwebs from his head which were put there by that devastating left hook from Henry Cooper.

In round five, Clay really laid into Cooper and ultimately hit him with a right hand that opened a horrible cut over Cooper's eye. But, then, that was not anything new, for Henry Cooper was well known as a serious bleeder. The referee took a good look and he decided that it was just too dangerous for

Henry Cooper to continue with such a bad cut. The fight was stopped - in round 5 - as Clay had predicted.

Part 6 HEAVYWEIGHT CHAMPIONSHIP FIGHT

It was time. Cassius Clay, the now 22-year-old brash Olympic boxing champion was the #1 contender. He had earned his right to a heavyweight championship fight, in search of the most coveted honor in all of boxing, the Heavyweight Championship of the World. But the current Champion, Sonny Liston, did not quite see it that way. He saw it as the time to shut the mouth of this bragging, overconfident young kid who had dared to show up with the attention of the media at Liston's house at 2:00 in the morning to challenge him to a title match. And as far as most people saw it, Liston had all that was necessary to shut Clay's mouth for good.

Sonny Liston was one of the most vicious punchers of all time. He would often intimidate his opponent before the opening bell with a face-to-face stare-down while the referee was giving last minute instructions. He had a prison record and was even once arrested for beating up a police officer. He had won all of his previous fights except one in which he had been injured. Most of his wins came by knockouts as his opponents could not withstand his awesome punching power. He met two-time title holder Floyd Patterson in their first heavyweight championship fight and knocked Patterson, the champion, out in just one round. Patterson, who was a brave and gallant champion, felt he just got nailed and decided to get the title back from Liston in a rematch, hoping to do much better the next time. So he earned another heavyweight championship fight, this time with Liston as the Champion. But Liston was so powerful, that he once again dispelled of Patterson by a knockout in the first round and everyone now knew that Sonny Liston was no champion to be taken lightly.

According to many in the Press, Clay didn't stand a single chance. Most predicted that Liston would knock Clay out either in the first or second round. Clay was promptly listed as a 7-1 underdog. Only two writers in all of the known Press gave Clay even a remote possibility of winning. This did not, however, stop the young Cassius from boldly displaying confidence that he would defeat Sonny Liston and win the Heavyweight Championship of the World. And he would never fail to let the press and the public know just how confident he was. He even put together a humorous poem to predict the outcome. Young Cassius said:

"Now those of you who won't be able to see the Clay-Liston

fight, here is the eighth round exactly as it will happen:

Clay comes out to meet Liston, and Liston starts to retreat,

If Liston goes back any farther, he'll end up in a ringside seat.

Clay swings with his left, Clay swings with his right,

Look at young Cassius carry the fight.

Liston keeps backing, but there's not enough room,

It's a matter of time – Oh, Clay lowers the boom!

Now Liston disappears from view; the crowd is getting frantic,

But our radar stations have picked him up, he is somewheres'

over the Atlantic.

Liston is still rising and the ref wears a frown,

For he can't stand counting 'till Sonny comes down.

Who would have thought when they came to the fight,

That they'd witness the launching of a human satellite?"

This was the kind of humor, fun and confidence which exuded from such a young, but talented, boxer as Cassius Clay was.

The weigh-in for this heavyweight championship fight was the most bizarre in all of boxing history. Cassius decided that he would try to psyche out the reigning Heavyweight Champ by letting him know, in no uncertain terms, that he could not be beaten. Sonny Liston had come into the arena accompanied by former Heavyweight great Joe Louis. So Clay came into the place and boldly announced, *"You tell Sonny Liston that I'm here with Sugar Ray!"* [Referring to former boxing champion Sugar Ray Robinson] *"We're two pretty dancers and we can't be beat!"* At the weigh-in, itself, Clay loudly and wildly proclaimed to Liston and to all that Sonny would fall in 8. Sonny, in the meantime, calmly and quietly held up two fingers - signifying that Clay wouldn't last through round two. The doctor examining Clay said that his blood pressure was very high, due to his frantic behavior, yelling at Liston about how he didn't stand a chance. His carrying on was so bad that Cassius was fined for misconduct. But he seemed intent on one thing only - to make Sonny Liston think he was about to face a madman loaded with confidence that just could not be beaten. Would Cassius Clay's psychological tactics work?

At long last, it was time for the heavyweight championship fight. The date was February 25, 1964. The place was Miami Beach, Florida. This was for the Heavyweight title belt. But no big deal, it seemed, for powerful Sonny Liston, thought most, would quickly do away with "Gaseous Cassius", the "Louisville Lip", the young, loud-mouthed kid.

Finally the fight began and, by the end of round 1, in which Cassius demonstrated superior defense, speed of hand and the ability to keep Liston off-balance, some could see that this bragging kid could not only talk a good fight, but he could fight a good fight, as well. The second and third rounds were shocking to the writers, boxing analysts, and Liston supporters, for Clay dominated Liston with his superior ring craftsmanship and youthful speed. He opened a cut under Liston's left eye, so by the end of round 3, Liston's cornermen were scurrying to stop the bleeding. They used an illegal substance called Monsel's Solution which, either accidentally or intentionally, got onto Liston's glove and, somehow throughout round 4, worked its way into Clay's eyes. When Clay returned to his corner to rest before round 5, his eyes were burning, he was blinking badly, and was in a state of panic because he could not see and cried 'dirty work' on someone's part. But his trainer, Angelo Dundee, told him that this was a heavyweight championship fight, and it was for all the marbles.

He gave Clay one instruction as the bell to begin Round 5 sounded - "RUN!"

Thankfully, Cassius Clay was a master of defense and was able, most of the time, to keep away from the now charging Sonny Liston. But Liston still managed to rain heavy blows on Clay's body and was doing his best to knock out the now blinded Clay. Some cried foul, as the previously dominating young boxer was now suddenly running for his life in the ring. Nevertheless, his speed prevailed, and by the middle of round 5 his eyes had begun to clear, allowing him to resume his domination of the slower, now less-confident Champion. Clay survived the scare of round 5 and then, in round 6, he again jabbed Liston at will and hit him in ways that Liston had never been hit before. His superiority in the ring clearly showed itself at this point and, by the end of round 6, Sonny Liston was a beaten champion. He told his handlers that he could not lift his arm, claiming a shoulder injury. A seemingly invincible Champion sat dejectedly on his stool, humbled in defeat.

As the bell sounded for Round 7, Cassius Clay had already raised his arms and shuffled his feet for he knew, somehow before everyone else, that Liston was not coming out to continue and that he was now the NEW Heavyweight

Champion of the World. Pandemonium broke out as Cassius Clay jumped around the ring to yell at the reporters and chide them as to just how wrong they had been. He had proven the experts, the analysts and the doubters wrong. He had done the unthinkable. He had won this heavyweight championship fight against the 7-1 odds. He had, as he put it, *"Shook up the World!"*

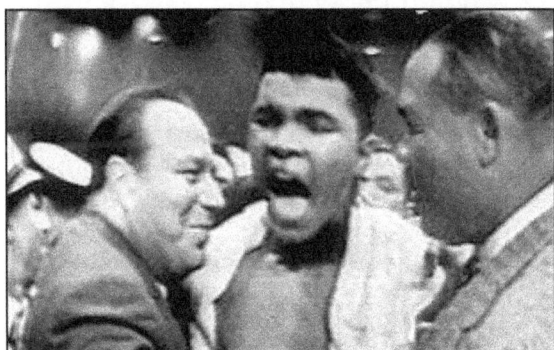

Source: AP

In the interview following his heavyweight championship fight, Clay yells emphatically, "I shook up the world! I shook up the world!"

Part 7 REMATCH / ALI-LISTON II

Cassius Clay was now the Heavyweight Champion of the World, as far as most people knew. But what was known by only a few was that the name of the champion would be changing again, just as quickly as it had by Liston's defeat. Cassius Clay had joined Elijah Muhammad's Nation of Islam and was now going to let the world know that he was a Muslim, and would henceforth be known as Muhammad Ali - "Muhammad" meaning *"Praiseworthy"* and "Ali" meaning *"Lofty, or High"*. This came as a big shock to many in America, partly because many didn't know what a Muslim was, partly because some who knew of Elijah Muhammad's teachings were offended or disturbed by it, and partly because some just didn't like the idea of the world's boxing champion claiming to be a Muslim. All of these factors began to stir the press and its gullible public into a frenzy of anti-Muhammad Ali feelings, words, and actions. It would set into motion the events that, over the next 20 years, would propel Muhammad Ali from one of the most hated and despised athletes in American history into one of America's, and the world's, all-time greatest heroes.

Being the Heavyweight Champion of the World, Muhammad Ali now had to begin defending his title against all who would like to be the next world's champ. On the very top of that list was none other than the recently dethroned Heavyweight Champ, Sonny Liston. Liston badly wanted to get back the title he had forsaken by sitting humbly on his stool in Round 7 on that infamous night of February 25, 1964. Ali, being the gentleman that he would always be, gladly obliged Liston by giving him the first shot at the title. Ali-Liston II was set to take place in November, 1964.

A couple of critical events, however, would forestall Liston's desired rematch. First, a few days before the fight, Muhammad Ali would suddenly be rushed to the hospital because he had ruptured a hernia. He had to receive an emergency operation. Quite naturally, this created a big delay in the fight. Liston, who claimed to now be in the best shape of his life - a difficult feat at his age - was understandably upset at this setback. But what happened next would be even worse. Some say it would even affect the outcome of the fight. Malcolm X, the fiery orator, was gunned down in February of 1965 in New York City. Malcolm had parted with Elijah Muhammad, Ali's leader, over a number of differences. Muhammad Ali took sides with Elijah Muhammad, so there was a parting of the ways between him and Malcolm. It appeared that Malcolm X's assassination was carried out by members of Elijah's Nation of Islam, with whom Muhammad Ali was still totally affiliated. Now being one of the Nation of Islam's most public figures, Ali's life was in jeopardy over possible retaliation from Malcolm's followers (at least as was rumored by the press - or maybe even those in higher positions of power). These disturbing events greatly diminished the desire of many promoters to put on an Ali-Liston fight, during which any number of things, it was feared, could break out. It became very difficult to find a venue for the fight, so Liston's desired rematch had to wait even longer. Finally, a date was set for May 25, 1965 and the venue was Lewiston, Maine.

The long-awaited rematch between Sonny Liston and Muhammad Ali would now take place. This fight would prove, many thought, that Ali's defeat of Liston was a fluke. Besides that, Ali, being a Muslim now, was much more unpopular in the public eye. Nothing would please them more than to see this loud-mouthed Muslim proven wrong about his claimed superiority over Liston and every other fighter. Muhammad Ali, on the other hand, wanted to show the world that not only had the first fight shown his superior skills, but this second one would prove it conclusively, by boxing Liston into submission over several rounds. Neither the public nor Muhammad Ali, however, would get their wish on this evening.

The fight began with Muhammad Ali moving, even more fluently, in his patented "Float Like a Butterfly" style, and stinging Liston with several quick, unanswered blows. Ali looked to be a bit stronger than he was in the first fight. It appeared that he would get to show the world just how superior he was to Liston, the once-thought unbeatable force in boxing. But almost two minutes into the fight, Ali hit Liston with a quick, overhand right which sent Liston crumbling to the canvas. Liston did not get up until about 14 seconds after the knockdown (thanks to some confusion caused by Ali yelling at Liston to *"Get up!"*).

After a bit more confusion, the fight resumed, and then was

quickly stopped again by referee and former boxer, Jersey Joe Walcott. The fight was declared over, with Ali the winner by knockout. It would be one of the strangest and most controversial knockouts in all of boxing history.

Several theories would emerge to try and explain this knockout win by Ali. The first is that it was a hard right that Liston did not see, which hit him flush on the temple. This kind of punch to the temple can, in fact, cause the sort of dizzy reaction that Liston seemed to exhibit after that punch, and even after the fight was stopped. Another theory is that Liston was afraid, because of the Ali death threats, that an attempt could actually have taken place against Ali's life and that Liston could be hit by a stray bullet. Some said, therefore, that he wanted out and took it the easy way, with a first-round KO. A third theory is that Liston, who had been known to have mob ties, could have taken a dive for money. About the theory of Liston taking a dive, Muhammad Ali once said, *"He did take a dive - - when I hit him with a right hand."* Whatever the reason, whether by Ali's licks or a Liston fix, the fight was over, and Sonny Liston had lost his bid to regain the title by a first-round KO. Charles "Sonny" Liston would never contend for the title again.

Part 8 TITLE DEFENSES

Muhammad Ali had now twice disposed of the big, bad Sonny Liston. He was indeed the undisputed Heavyweight Champion of the World. It was time to move on and begin to defend his title against others who wanted a shot at the championship belt. His next opponent would be the man who held the title of Heavyweight Champion before Sonny Liston, the former two-time champ, Floyd Patterson. This fight would also bring in problems for Ali. Floyd Patterson claimed that he would fight Muhammad Ali for free. His reason was that the Heavyweight Championship belonged to the American people not just to the "Black" Muslims. This infuriated Ali, along with the fact that Patterson refused to call him Muhammad Ali, but insisted, instead, on calling him "Clay". An animosity built up between the two men, and Ali warned Patterson that he would give him a good "whupping".

The fight took place on November 22, 1965, in Las Vegas, Nevada. Ali used the first few rounds to dominate Patterson with his superior ring skills. As the fight carried on and Ali began to really beat up on Patterson, it became apparent that Ali was the better fighter and that Patterson was a beaten man. But many people criticized him, saying that instead of Ali knocking Patterson out, which he probably could have done, he held back and chose, instead, to put a whipping on Patterson for all that had been said. Ali, on the other hand, has always stated that if the referee had thought Patterson was so badly hurt, he could have stopped the fight at any point. That being the case, the referee stepped in during the 12th round and claimed that Patterson had taken enough. Again, Muhammad Ali had shown that he was the best fighter in the world.

Muhammad Ali's next fight would begin outside of the ring. In March of 1964, Ali had been classified by the draft board as 1-Y, which meant he was ineligible for the draft. Two months after his battle with Patterson, the draft board suddenly decided to reclassify Ali as 1-A, making him eligible for the draft. Muhammad Ali had become Muslim, and his religion was opposed to being drafted into the United States Army. It would seem that Ali was being fought against both inside the ring and outside the ring. He then created a whirlwind in an interview when he stated, in reference to being drafted to go and fight in Vietnam, *"I ain't got no quarrel with them Vietcong."* This statement, which the press turned into front-page news, sent shockwaves through some people, as if Ali was supposed to automatically see Vietnamese people as his enemy. Not every person is ready to go and kill people not even known to him, and Muhammad Ali, who was a very peaceful man outside of the ring, just happened to be one of those people. Like many, many others in America, Ali claimed that he was opposed to war in general, and the Vietnam war in particular, and was therefore opposed to being drafted and sent to Vietnam. He claimed that it was against his religious beliefs, and it was. He was sincere in his stance, but was immediately ostracized and criticized and bombarded with trouble from an unsympathetic public that was being led by the nose through the press.

Needless to say, it became much more difficult to book a boxing match for Muhammad Ali in the United States after he let his position on the Vietnam War be known. His proposed fight with top-ranked Ernie Terrell could not be negotiated anywhere because no one wanted to deal with protests surrounding Muhammad Ali. Was it the war stance, or was it the objections to his religion? Either way, the plans for the Terrell fight fell apart, and Ali's next fight finally took place in Canada, March 29, 1966, against rugged George Chuvalo. It turned out to be a 15-round battle, with Ali winning handily, but not gaining any better support from the American public.

He had become strongly disliked, so his people decided it might be better to get out of the U.S. for awhile.

Over the next 6 months, Ali would travel to England and Germany and would be received like a hero. Thousands of people would gather in the streets just to get a glimpse of the reigning World's Heavyweight Champion. He was well loved and appreciated by an adoring public in England. So Muhammad Ali's promoters were able to easily book a boxing match against England's own Henry Cooper, the fighter who almost put Ali's lights out with a left hook some two years earlier. This next title defense would take place on May 21, 1966 in London, and Ali would once again stop Cooper on a vicious cut, this time in the 6th round.

Next up for Muhammad Ali was Brian London, a well-known and popular English fighter. This fight would take place on August 6, 1966 in London, as well, and Muhammad Ali would take out Brian London in the third round, with probably the most gorgeous combination of punches you'll ever see in a boxing match. With this defeat of Brian London, Ali had now successfully defended his Heavyweight title five times, and his overall record was now 25-0.

For the sixth defense of his title, Ali would now take on Germany's Karl Mildenberger. This fight would take place in Frankfurt, Germany, and would be the first time that a German would fight for the Heavyweight title in Germany since Max Schmeling, way back in the Joe Louis era. Karl Mildenberger was a game fighter and his fighting style would sometimes trouble the champion. But Ali proved too much for his German opponent and the fight would end with a 12th round TKO victory by Muhammad Ali.

Meanwhile, boxing promoters in the United States began to see how much they were missing out on big, money-making events by not having the Heavyweight Champion fighting in the States. So finally, one of them relented, and decided to sponsor a fight with "The Big Cat", Cleveland Williams, in Houston, Texas. The fight took place on November 14, 1966, an entire 11 months since Ali's last fight in the United States. This fight would, in my opinion, show Muhammad Ali at his very best ever, probably the most dominant demonstration of his entire career. In this one fight you saw Ali's lightning fast footwork, hand speed and knockout power (which his critics always tried to claim he did not have) all coming one after another.

Cleveland Williams had, up to that point, one of the most impressive knockout records in boxing history. Yet this powerful fighter was so completely overwhelmed by this great champion of boxing that it was absolutely no contest. In an awesome display of skill and power, Muhammad Ali completely destroyed Cleveland Williams, knocking him down several times with vicious combinations, and eventually winning by a third-round knockout.

Part 9 ERNIE TERRELL - MORE CONTROVERSY

At long last, there was a match set between Muhammad Ali and Ernie Terrell. The fight would take place on February 6, 1967, in Houston, Texas. There were many who felt that Ernie Terrell would give Ali lots of trouble as he was taller than Ali and was undefeated in his last 15 fights. But Terrell did not let his chances rest on that, alone. He figured that he would try to get "under Ali's skin" by referring to him only as Cassius Clay and not as Muhammad Ali. So tensions built up prior to fight time. Soon after the fight began, Terrell claimed that he had received an injury to his eye, producing double-vision. He tried to say that Ali had done this intentionally with his thumb, but Ali denied this, and replays have never shown anything to substantiate Terrell's claim. Nevertheless, Muhammad Ali managed to beat up on Ernie Terrell pretty badly in the first seven rounds. In the eighth round, a dramatic occurrence took place as Ali began to land vicious combinations on Terrell and would ask him, *"What's my name?"* This was done a few times and then, when the bell rang to end round eight, Ali stood in ring center and shouted angrily at Terrell, *"What's my name, huh? - - What's my name?!"*

Due to this angry outburst, along with the beating that Terrell would take over the next 7 rounds, the press (again) and the public condemned Ali as being vicious and cruel, beating on a man "who couldn't see". Muhammad Ali appeared on TV with Howard Cosell to dispel much of the controversy that this fight brought about, by showing that Terrell reacted when punches were thrown at him as if he was quite able to see, and also that he retaliated throughout the entire fight, causing Ali to still have to defend himself. As Ali said, *"Either I was going to hit him or he was going to hit me."* As always, it seemed, Muhammad Ali came out the winner as a boxer, but the loser as a public figure. But the worse was yet to come.

His next fight was scheduled for March 22, 1967 against Zora Folley. About two weeks before the fight, his 1-A classification was upheld by an Appeal Board, meaning that he was officially and completely eligible for the draft. Muhammad Ali knew that he was not going to accept to be drafted, so he began to say in interviews that this upcoming fight with Zora Folley would probably be his last. When March 22nd came, Ali met Folley in Madison Square Garden in New York City, and Ali was in top form, although he probably had more than just this fight on his mind. In the fourth round, Ali landed a sharp right hand which sent Folley to the canvas. Folley was able to get up, so the fight resumed. It carried on for another couple of rounds until, in round 7, Ali once again hit Folley with two straight, quick right hands which sent Folley down, and out, and Muhammad Ali had won a 7th round knockout. Unfortunately, the boxing world would never again see Muhammad Ali fight at this level of speed and energy after this night, for Ali would be called up for induction into the United States military 35 days after his fight with Zora Folley. This next battle for Muhammad Ali would be the toughest of all.

Part 10 THE DRAFT AND EXILE OF ALI

On April 28, 1967, Muhammad Ali reported to the Induction Center, where his name would be called for induction into the U.S. Army. When your name is called, it is your duty, so says the law, to take one step forward from the line. This simple act signifies your acceptance of the draft and admission into the military. But Muhammad Ali was no simple personality. When the officer called his name, he refused to step forward and acknowledge the draft. The procedure, when this happens, calls for the person to be removed from the room, warned of the consequences of such action, returned to the room and have his name called once again, giving him a second chance to step forward and accept the draft. When this was done, Muhammad Ali refused, once again, to step forward. He would not accept to be inducted into the U.S. military. This refusal would create a storm of events that would last for many years to come.

Immediately, in as little as one hour, the New York State Athletic Commission stripped Muhammad Ali of his title. All of the other United States Boxing Commissions did the same. For refusing to accept the draft and join the military, on religious grounds, Muhammad Ali was no longer considered the

Heavyweight Champion of the World. State Athletic Commissions all over the United States suspended Muhammad Ali's boxing license, making it illegal for him to box in the U.S. Slightly more than a week later, a federal grand jury in Houston, Texas would indict Ali on refusal to be inducted. His trial began in June and it took only two days for Muhammad Ali to be found guilty of refusing induction into the Armed Forces, given a sentence of five years in prison, and a $10,000 fine. The final knockout blow came by the judge who then took Ali's passport away from him, so that now he could not travel and could not, therefore, fight anywhere in the world. It was only by his lawyer's' appeal that Ali was kept from actually going to prison. He was let go on bail. But boxing matches were no longer permissible for Muhammad Ali.

At this point, Muhammad Ali was 25 years old, had no income and had mounting legal fees. Despite this, he stood by his convictions, sacrificing millions of dollars to keep his principles. Whenever the issue of the draft was brought up, and the question of penalties for standing up for his religious beliefs was raised, Muhammad Ali was prepared to face it. As he said, *"Even if it means standing up to machine-gun fire, before renouncing my religion, I'm ready to die."* The situation with Muhammad Ali and the draft had become extremely serious, and had brought him to a low point in his life. And, mercifully, it was at this low point that he met Belinda Boyd, who soon agreed to marry him. Ali's first marriage to Sonji Roi had ended in divorce, so Belinda, soon to be known as Khalilah Ali, would become Muhammad Ali's second wife, and would bring some joy and relief to such a troubled man.

It was also at this time that Ali began to give talks on college campuses and would earn money from those lectures. He became very good at these talks and would soon be in great demand. So, although Muhammad Ali could not fight at this stage, he still was able to at least earn some money through another of his talents -- talking. But with an impending conviction for Muhammad Ali and having the draft issue hanging over his head, Ali still had many money problems. Some of the things he did to generate income were a documentary, called A.K.A. Cassius Clay, a computer-generated fight between himself and former undefeated Heavyweight Champion Rocky Marciano, and to do a Broadway Musical called "Buck White".

As time passed in 1968, with the assassinations of Martin Luther King, Jr. and Robert Kennedy, Woodstock and the Watts riots, the sentiments in America were taking an entirely different turn. By 1969, it seemed that most of the young people in America, and many older Americans, as well, were strongly against the Vietnam War and the draft, just as Muhammad Ali had been. Muhammad Ali had suddenly become a spokesman and a figure-head for protesters against the War. His popularity took a strong upturn, and he was seen on many TV talk-shows and even a few game shows. Then in 1970, a major breakthrough occurred. After trying for over three years to convince someone to sponsor a fight for Muhammad Ali and being unsuccessful because Ali had no boxing license and, thus, could never get sanction from any State Athletic Commission, a State Legislator in Georgia named Leroy Johnson successfully convinced others in the state to allow a fight to take place. The great loophole was that the State of Georgia did not have a State Athletic Commission. With the help of the Mayor, Muhammad Ali was, at long last, signed to fight once again, this time against Jerry Quarry in Atlanta, Georgia on October 26, 1970, exactly three years and six months after he boldly refused to step forward in Houston, Texas. After having previously announced that he would no longer fight again because he believed no boxing match would ever be allowed for him, and thereby virtually retiring from the ring by making such an announcement, the great champion, Muhammad Ali, was back where he rightfully belonged.

Part 11   THE RETURN OF MUHAMMAD ALI

On a glorious night in October of 1970, Muhammad Ali stepped through the ropes to a tremendous roar from the crowd in a triumphant return to the boxing ring. He was no longer recognized by the authorities of boxing as the champion, but he was "The People's Champion". He had not lost his title in the ring, but had it taken from him unjustly by a biased and prejudiced system that refused to recognize a man's right to his beliefs. So now, thanks to a loophole in that same system and the pulling of some strings, Ali would now begin his quest to regain what he felt was his all along -- the Heavyweight Championship of the World. And that quest would begin this night, in Atlanta, Georgia, against a game and crafty fighter named Jerry Quarry.

Quarry had lost a bid to be champ himself in an elimination tournament that was held during the layoff of Muhammad Ali. Jimmy Ellis, managed by Angelo Dundee, defeated Quarry to win the WBA version of the title, while Joe Frazier knocked out Buster Mathis to win the WBC version. In a unification bout, Joe Frazier would emerge victorious, with a knockout victory over Jimmy Ellis, and be declared the undisputed Champion.

So Jerry Quarry was a top contender, and no easy opponent. And Muhammad Ali only had six weeks to prepare for this fight. The fight began, and Ali floated and stung in typical Ali fashion, so beautifully that it almost looked as though he had never been away from boxing. There were, however, very subtle changes in him, now being three and a half years older than he was in his last fight and not fighting for 43 months. This kind of layoff takes its toll on any athlete, whether in boxing, basketball, or badminton. Still, Ali won the first round supremely. The second round showed Ali with his ring mastery giving Quarry a very difficult time by constantly beating him to the punch, but also slowing down just a bit, probably due to the long layoff. He still, however, seemed in very good shape as far as the fight was progressing. In the third round, each man exchanged blows until, suddenly, the two clashed together and Jerry Quarry received a horrible cut over his eye which bled quite badly. Even though he had a very good cut man in his corner, his people and the doctor decided it was too risky for Quarry to continue. The fight was stopped, and Muhammad Ali had won by a third round TKO in his return match. He was still undefeated, at 30-0. The return of the champion had begun.

Part 12 MUHAMMAD ALI vs. OSCAR BONAVENA

Ali was anxious to get to the reigning Champion, Joe Frazier, so that he could show the world that he, Muhammad Ali, was the real champion since his title had not been taken in the ring. But his fight with Quarry had only gone three rounds, clearly not enough real combat to prepare him for a title match. So it was decided that Ali would take on a rough, tough, brawling Argentinean named Oscar Bonavena. Like Quarry, Bonavena was no newcomer on the scene. He had vast ring experience and had done battle with Joe Frazier in a match which Bonavena lost, but still managed to knock Joe Frazier down a couple of times. He was a solid puncher, and figured to give Ali a rough time in the ring. The fight would take place on December 7, 1970, exactly 6 weeks since Ali's return match with Jerry Quarry.

Like Floyd Patterson and Ernie Terrell had done years before him, Oscar Bonavena decided to try and get underneath Ali's skin prior to the fight. He called Ali "chicken" for not going to the War. He called him "Clay" for the express purpose of annoying Muhammad Ali. He even said that he wanted the 3 knockdown rule waived so that he could keep knocking

Muhammad Ali down continuously. He stirred up the situation enough for Muhammad Ali to go back to what he used to do so well -- recite poetry about his upcoming opponent.

Here is a portion of what Ali had to say about Bonavena and his mouthing-off:

"It's been a long time

since I've put my predictions in rhythm and rhyme.

But it was Bonavena who started it all

By getting out of line.

He's asked the commission to waive the three-knockdown rule.

He must be crazy, or maybe a fool.

I understand he wants the rules changed to make me suffer,

but he'll be all shook up when he finds out I'm tougher.

He has a dream - - he wants to punish me,

but has he forgotten he's fighting Muhammad Ali?"

The fight began and Ali began well as he always had and scored early points against Bonavena. But Bonavena had a very unusual, bullying style of fighting and this awkwardness kept Ali's timing off balance for a good part of the fight. It became a different kind of a fight for Ali, not the usual floating and stinging tactics previously employed throughout his entire career. This was more of a warring, battling Muhammad Ali, often flat-footed and slugging it out with Bonavena. For those expecting to see Ali at his best, this fight seemed disappointing. To many, the fight even seemed close going into the 15th and final round. For boxing fans, it seemed uneventful until, suddenly, from out of nowhere, Muhammad Ali threw a vicious left hook which caught Bonavena on the jaw and sent him sprawling to the canvas. Bonavena was in big trouble. He got up and Ali hit him with two or three more blows and he went down a second time. It seemed as if poor Oscar Bonavena was right -- they should have waived the three knockdown rule, for it was *he*, not Muhammad Ali, for whom the rule might now come into play. After getting up again, Ali pursued him, hit him again with two or three more blows, and Bonavena hit the canvas for the third time. The fight was over. Muhammad Ali had scored a knockout victory over the tough Oscar Bonavena, who had lost by the very rule he wanted waived. This 15th round would be remembered by boxing fans for many, many years to come. Muhammad Ali was back for sure.

Part 13   "THE FIGHT" - ALI vs. FRAZIER I

It was time -- at least as far as Muhammad Ali was concerned. Joe Frazier was the Champion. Ali felt that he was the true Champion, not Frazier. Many agreed. Many disagreed. But what was certain was that Frazier had never been defeated. And Muhammad Ali had never been defeated. There were two undefeated Heavyweight Champions claiming the title at the same time. Never in the annals of boxing had such a situation existed. The stage was set for a showdown. It would be Muhammad Ali at 31-0 against "Smokin' Joe" Frazier at 26-0. The date was set for March 8, 1971. Each fighter would receive $2,500,000 -- the largest payday for any fight in boxing history at that time.

For sure, Joe Frazier would be no pushover. After all, he had won the elimination tournament held during Ali's absence from the ring. And he won it convincingly, with vicious knockouts of both Buster Mathis and Jimmy Ellis. He was known for a vicious left hook which he used to full advantage in both of those knockout victories. His opponent, however, was Ali -- and some were already saying that he may have been the greatest of all time. But others were more cautious in their opinions, for Ali had been off for three-and-a-half years while Frazier was in his top form. Frazier said that the fight wouldn't go the distance; that he would stop Ali within 10 rounds. Ali, on the other hand, said that it would be *"No Contest"*, meaning that Frazier would not be able to keep up with Ali's boxing superiority. The buildup for this fight was tremendous, with newspapers sometimes giving front, center and back-page coverage of commentaries, comparisons and predictions. The excitement would make it one of the greatest sporting events of all time, and the fight, itself, would help to solidify that opinion. On the evening of March 8, 1971, a capacity crowd of fans and celebrities filled New York's Madison Square Garden for what would be one of the most anticipated boxing matches in history. It would decide, once and for all, who was the undisputed Heavyweight Champion of the World.

At long last, it was fight time. Round 1. Ali vs. Frazier. Muhammad came out quickly and began to throw jabs at Frazier who was bobbing and weaving in his trademark style referred to as "Smoking", while constantly moving towards Muhammad Ali. Ali would throw jabs and rights at Frazier to try and keep him at bay. Frazier would unleash a couple of his vicious left hooks at Ali, which Ali claimed didn't hurt him.

Both men fought furiously in that first round, and many say that it was one of the greatest first rounds ever seen in boxing.

Rounds two through five somewhat kept the same pace and direction as the first round with scorers giving at least 4 of those rounds to Ali. Things seemed to be going Ali's way as Frazier was not off to a very quick start. But Frazier was always a slow starter, however, he would eventually start to 'smoke'. His hooks began to find their mark on Ali, and his constant pressure began to wear at Muhammad as Frazier continuously cut off Ali from movement around the ring. Ali was not able to float and dance as was his trademark style. His tactic for this fight was to fend off an on-rushing Joe Frazier, who was relentless in his bobbing and weaving and moving in for vicious body shots and occasional hooks to Muhammad Ali's jaw. The tide was beginning to turn slowly in Frazier's favor as he would win several of the middle rounds and begin to even up the fight.

And what a fight it had become! Two heavyweights, both champions in their own right, slugging it out round by round. Ali would take over and turn things his way, then Frazier would take over and gain the momentum. Back and forth. Then, in the 11th round, Ali decided to play with Frazier as he had once or twice in some previous rounds and, towards the end of the round, was suddenly rocked with a vicious left hook from Frazier. Ali's legs went rubbery and he fell back into the ropes, then staggered and bounced around the ring to try and avoid more damage from Frazier who was looking for the kill. But after about 30 seconds of danger for Ali, time ran out for Frazier in the round, and Ali was saved by the bell, barely escaping a knockout.

After such a disastrous round for Ali, being badly shaken, you would think that everything would be all in Frazier's favor from here. But again, Ali showed his greatness and would be the better fighter over the next couple of rounds, an amazing feat at any point but more so at the late stages of such a grueling fight. But then, there was round 15, the final round. Both men felt that they needed to win this round. It was a very important round for it would leave the final imprint in the minds of the judges. This is where Ali could show the judges his superiority, dance and stick, float and sting and come out victorious. But not this night. Out of nowhere, after a clinch, Frazier reared back and threw a haymaker of a left hook which landed flush on Muhammad Ali's chin, sending Ali flat on his back. It would be a knockdown remembered for years to come, and it was Frazier's defining moment, probably the greatest of his career. It would also be remembered because it was the perfect knockout punch, yet Ali, instead of being out for the count, would be up by the count of 3. This was greatness, even in a losing cause. Ali would last out the round and even put on a small rally of his own. But when it was all over, "Smoking" Joe Frazier had won a unanimous decision and retained the title. Muhammad Ali had lost for the first time in his career.

While many who did not like Ali celebrated his loss, Muhammad Ali took this first defeat like a man. He knew that everyone has to face a defeat sometimes in life and it was time for him to face one. He told the world that he would come back, and told Joe Frazier, *"You know, Joe, we've got to go one more time!"* Even in defeat, Muhammad Ali had earned the respect of his critics, and they now knew that Ali was a great fighter. He had lost on points but had fought a tremendous and courageous fight. This time Ali came out the loser as a boxer but a winner in the public eye.

Part 14 THE SECOND JOURNEY

Muhammad Ali had lost. There was no longer any question about it -- Ali was not the Heavyweight Champion of the World. Joe Frazier was. So what was Ali to do now? Would he retire? Would he simply go away and not be heard from again? This was not the character of Muhammad Ali. He decided he would get back into the swing of things, move ahead, and claw his way back to the title once again. His journey to the title had ended with the biggest defeat of his career, and his second journey would begin with the biggest win of his life. But this win would take place outside of the ring. On June 28, 1971, just three months after his loss to Joe Frazier, the Supreme Court voted 8-0 to overturn his conviction on draft evasion charges. Muhammad Ali was once again a free man. He was given his passport and was now free to travel anywhere in the world he would like. And travel he did. He would go to Nigeria, Italy, Switzerland, and England. In January of 1972, he would travel to Mecca, Saudi Arabia, to make the Hajj or Pilgrimage.

During this time, though, Muhammad Ali would also manage to have three fights in between. He would defeat Jimmy

Ellis, Buster Mathis and Jurgen Blin. After his travels, he would then fight and defeat Mac Foster, George Chuvalo, Jerry Quarry, Al Lewis, Floyd Patterson and Bob Foster. All these fights were preparations for what he really wanted -- another shot at the title.

Part 15 THE SETBACK

Joe Frazier was still the Champion, and Muhammad Ali wanted to avenge his loss and wrest the title away from "Smoking Joe". But two events would occur which would forever keep Ali from taking the title away from Joe Frazier. One was that Joe Frazier would meet a relatively unknown fighter named George Foreman in Kingston, Jamaica on January 22, 1973 and, shockingly, would be knocked down 6 times in the first two rounds before the referee mercifully stopped the slaughter and George Foreman was the NEW Heavyweight Champion of the World. The other event was that, after Foreman became champion, Ali defeated Joe Bugner and then fought a not-yet-well-known boxer named Ken Norton on March 31, 1973 and would catch a vicious overhand right flush on the jaw in Round 2 which would break Ali's jaw. But instead of Ali stopping and going to the hospital to repair his jaw, he continued on with the fight against the wishes of Angelo Dundee and Dr. Ferdie Pacheco, and would endure what must have been excruciating pain over another 10 long rounds, only to lose by a decision.

This was an amazing fighter and an amazing man. Most fighters would not have been able to withstand the pain of an inch-and-a-half break in the jawbone, alone, much less continuing to get hit in that area, as Ali did. Muhammad Ali withstood it, and still fought gallantly. But here he suffered the second defeat of his career and was now even further away from the heavyweight title than ever before. Some said that this was the end for Muhammad Ali. But they didn't know that this was only a setback on an amazing journey that would shock the world once again.

Ali had his jaw wired and had to talk through clenched teeth for awhile. During this time of healing, his people tried to negotiate a match with a boxer here and a boxer there for this amount of money and that amount, but Ali would not hear of it. He wanted one man. He wanted one fight. He wanted Ken Norton. He had to prove that it was the broken jaw that kept him from winning, not that he was through or washed up. So he was signed to a rematch with Norton. He trained and trained and got into the best shape he had been in for many years. And his jaw healed wonderfully. On September 10, 1973, about six months after the broken jaw, Muhammad Ali met Ken Norton to avenge his previous loss. This was another hard fought battle as Norton's "crab-like" movement and "peek-a-boo" style (like Archie Moore) gave Ali a lot of trouble. But Ali was not to be denied. He danced and floated and stung as he had in previous years and won the decision to avenge that broken-jaw loss to Ken Norton. Ali was now back on the road, back in contention for the title.

On January 28, 1974, Muhammad Ali met Joe Frazier with the intent of avenging his other previous loss, on that famous night in 1971 when Frazier won the 15 round decision. Both fighters were now ex-champions as Frazier had beaten Ali and Foreman had beaten Frazier. This fight would take place, just like their first meeting, in New York's Madison Square Garden. On this night, however, it would be a different Ali than Frazier had met in their first fight three years earlier. This was a better-conditioned Ali, no longer exhibiting ring rust from a three year layoff. Had it not been for a costly error by referee Tony Perez, this fight might have ended in round 2. In the second round, Ali hurt Frazier and had him in trouble. He was possibly a few punches away from going down when the referee stepped in and stopped the action, signifying that the round had ended. But there had been no bell, and Madison Square Garden had lights in the corner that lit when the round ended. No lights, and no bell, but Tony Perez sent both fighters to their corners, only to have them resume after 10 seconds or so, just enough time to let Frazier off the hook. Perez got in trouble with the boxing authorities for that mistake, Frazier got out of trouble by it, and Ali did not appreciate that mistake too well. The fight went the distance, and Ali won a unanimous 12-round decision. He had avenged his loss to Joe Frazier and was now ready to climb a huge mountain -- to go after the title presently held by big George Foreman.

Part 16   THE "RUMBLE IN THE JUNGLE"

George Foreman was the Heavyweight Champion of the World. And as far as the public, the boxing analysts and the press were concerned, Foreman was indestructible. At the time he held the greatest knockout percentage in all of boxing history. No one - - not Joe Frazier, who had gone the distance twice with Muhammad Ali, nor Ken Norton, who had also gone the distance twice with Muhammad Ali - - had managed to last more than three rounds with Foreman in the last several years. Foreman destroyed Ken Norton with a devastating knockout in the second round, so many people did not give Ali a good chance of defeating Foreman. Ali was now 32 years old and did not have the youth nor the punching power of George Foreman. But none of this dissuaded Ali. As always, he was loaded with confidence, and he said, *"George Foreman, lately, hasn't heard the man say 'Round Four', 'Round Seven', 'Round Nine', 'Round Thirteen', 'Last Round'.... Experience -- that's how I know I'll win."*

So the stage was set -- Ali vs. Foreman -- $5,000,000 apiece to fight for the Heavyweight Championship of the World, in Kinshasha, Zaire in Africa. While training, Foreman would receive a cut over his eye, which would delay the fight for six weeks, but after the initial disappointment of the postponement, Ali continued training until the day of the fight had drawn near.

The date was October 30, 1974 and many in the press, even long-time Ali supporter Howard Cosell, were eulogizing Ali as if he were going to get killed. Even some members of his own entourage secretly felt that Ali could not beat the indestructible Foreman. But Ali felt he could do it. And the support for Ali from the people of Zaire was overwhelming. From the time Ali had arrived in Africa, the people in the streets had raised, in loud cries, *"Ali, Bomaye!"*, which meant "Ali, Kill him!". Muhammad Ali seemed to draw strength from being in Africa and the total support of the people. So when fight time arrived, Ali was still quite confident of his chances. After all, he had been the veteran of many difficult battles. He was ready. But many did not know how he would handle this awesome challenge.

The time had come. Ali vs. Foreman for the Heavyweight Title. The fight began. Round 1. Immediately, Ali began this fight in a different way than what was expected. To survive against the powerful Foreman, most thought that Ali would begin by dancing, moving and staying away. But Ali came right at Foreman, hitting him with a shot to the head, and then carefully watching, defending, and striking at just the right moments. Everyone seemed to hold their breath because, after having seen Foreman destroy Frazier and Norton so easily, they expected that Foreman would land one of those massive punches and either knock out, hurt or kill Muhammad Ali. But Ali kept on fighting, and round one ended with Ali having gotten the best of Foreman in a glorious first round battle. In round two, Ali continued taking the fight to Foreman while simultaneously keeping Foreman from landing one of those vicious blows that ended all of his previous fights. But Ali began to see that floating and dancing would not be an option this night as it was a small ring with soft flooring, so he had to utilize a new tactic -- "The Rope-a-Dope" -- where he would begin to lay on the ropes and let Foreman shoot his best shots.

By round three, Foreman was intent on bringing this fight to a close, as he had done with everyone else he fought in the last few years. So he tried his best to set Ali up with body shots and then go to the head for the knockout blow. But Ali began laying back and taking Foreman's shots on the arms, blocking them from doing any real damage. Of course, when you have one of the most vicious punchers in the world wailing away at you, it will take its toll at some point, either now or later. But Ali hung in there, took Foreman's shots and he threw back a good number of blows as well. Near the end of each round, Ali would open up and attack Foreman with wicked jabs and right hand leads to the head which would snap Foreman's head back and make him reel. And all the while, Foreman was beginning to wear down as he was heading into round 4 -- territory that he hadn't seen in years. In that 4th round, Ali continued the same trend, blocking Foreman's punches and attacking when most appropriate. He was now frustrating George and as the minutes rolled by, Foreman was getting into deeper and deeper water.

In round 5, it seems Foreman had had enough of Muhammad Ali. George was the champ and he was not going to let Ali take his title -- so he thought. Round 5 was where George Foreman let loose and would wail away at Ali, who just sat back and let him throw at will. For Ali fans, it was a frightening, nail-biting spectacle as Foreman threw haymaker after haymaker against Ali's body and arms and tried taking his head off. It seemed only a matter of time before one of those shots would take Ali down and out for the count. But it didn't happen. Amazingly, with all of Foreman's power being exhibited in those punches, Ali kept talking to Foreman, saying to him, *"Is that as hard as you can hit, man?"* and telling Foreman that he wasn't hurting him.

So Muhammad Ali was frustrating George to the maximum while simultaneously wearing him out, then Ali would unleash a barrage of blows to shake Foreman up and leave him dizzy. This was a brilliant and tactical strategy being employed by Muhammad Ali and George Foreman was really beginning to show the effects by the end of round 5.

Now Foreman was into round 6 and was no longer used to fighting this much time in one match. He was wearing thin. His legs were no longer strong and his punches lacked the raw power that was so obvious in the early rounds of the fight. But Foreman always had enough power to take a fighter out at any point, so Ali had to continue being careful. Round 6 was another 3 minutes of desperation for Foreman and careful manipulation by Ali. Round 7 saw more of the same, but the heat and battle fatigue which had clearly worn down Foreman was beginning to wear on Ali, as well. Before the start of round 8, Ali told trainer Angelo Dundee, *"Foreman is tired...I think I can knock him out."* A still worried Angelo Dundee told Ali, *"Why don't you just do that!"*

In round 8, Ali let Foreman try his best shots with what energy he had left, and Ali just boxed and defended. With about a half minute left, Ali hit Foreman with a sharp right, then backed up and hit him with another one, then he threw a beautiful three or four punch combination of lefts and rights which sent Foreman spinning and reeling and trying to hold himself up...but it didn't work. The heavyweight champion was on the canvas as Ali walked to a neutral corner. The ref counted while Foreman struggled to get to his feet, but he didn't get up in time. The referee counted out George Foreman and once again, Muhammad Ali had shocked the world and was the NEW Heavyweight Champion of the World. He was now the second man in boxing history to regain the heavyweight title (Floyd Patterson was the first). Muhammad Ali had knocked out the knockout artist.

Ali's battle with Foreman turned out to be one of the biggest upsets in boxing history. The crowd in Zaire went wild and shock waves were felt worldwide over this great victory. It took him 7 years to reach his goal of reclaiming the elusive title which had been unjustly taken from him in 1967. At long last, Muhammad Ali was once again King of the boxing world.

Part 17 CHAMP ONCE AGAIN

Now that he had attained his goal, Muhammad Ali was in a good position to retire as champ if he chose to do so. But what seemed like the time for a good ending only became a new beginning. Not only was it now a good opportunity for other fighters to go after Ali for the title but, after a five million dollar payday in the Foreman fight, it became quite profitable to challenge Ali, also. So the offers began to roll in for Ali to fight different opponents, making it quite difficult for him to refuse and consider retirement. Finally, the first challenger chosen was a heavyweight named Chuck Wepner.

This did not turn out to be a classic fight, but Wepner's courage inspired a well-known actor, Sylvester Stallone, to develop a character called, "Rocky", for a movie which became a box-office success with several sequels. One moment in the Wepner fight does stand out as special, however. It was in one of the later rounds that Wepner hit Ali with a body shot and Ali went down. Ali claimed that he fell, but the referee ruled it a knockdown. Replays will show that Ali's foot and Wepner's foot came together at the time of the punch, so it seems that Ali was correct as it appears that he actually tripped on Wepner's foot.

Despite this incident and much hitting in the back of the head by Wepner, Ali pretty much won every round of the fight and stopped Wepner in the 15th round.

Ali would continue in his title defenses with wins against Ron Lyle and Joe Bugner. As the years were beginning to affect his skills, his fights would begin to get tougher and tougher and Ali would find training more and more difficult. As each fight approached, Ali would give more and more consideration to the idea of retirement. Some in his camp considered that to be a good idea, however, it did not bear fruit. There were still two more historic moments for the great Muhammad Ali to fulfill. The first of these would be the rubber match in the trilogy with former champ, "Smokin' Joe" Frazier.

Part 18 "THE THRILLER IN MANILA"

Muhammad Ali decided to give Frazier a shot at the title now that he was the champion. In their first fight, Frazier was the champion. In the second battle, neither fighter was the champion. Now Ali was the champ, so Frazier felt that he would once again wear the belt of the Heavyweight Champion of the World. The fight was signed for October 1, 1975 in Manila in the Philippines. It was Ali who would dub this battle as "The Thrilla' in Manila", and it would turn out to be very aptly named, for in the end this would be considered by many as one of the greatest fights of all time.

In round 1, Ali wanted to show that he was now much more superior to Frazier than ever before, because he was the Champ, he was more experienced than ever, and because he and his camp believed that Frazier was "over-the-hill" and this would be an easy fight. So Ali hit Frazier with a number of right hand leads, and at one point, Ali hit Frazier and knocked him off balance. The crowd went wild, as they saw Frazier stumble and Ali went after him methodically, possibly hoping to end the match early. But Frazier hung in and survived that first round flurry. Round 2 showed more of the same, with Ali winning the round handily and demonstrating superior hand speed by constantly beating Frazier to the punch and not taking much retaliation in return. Round 3 saw Ali use the "Rope-a-Dope" tactic which had worked with Foreman, and he used that until, suddenly, he opened up and both fighters went into a brutal exchange matching any you might see in boxing history, a toe-to-toe slugfest which carried on until the end of the round.

Then, as was Frazier's trademark pattern, he would begin to pick up steam as the rounds moved on, and by rounds 5 and 6, Frazier was "smoking" and catching Ali with those vicious body shots and left hooks that he was famous for. These body shots, along with the sweltering heat that had built up in the place, were beginning to take its toll on Ali, and Muhammad's blistering jabs, hooks, right hand leads and uppercuts were beginning to wear on Frazier. This fight would call on conditioning and, luckily, both men were in good condition. But the pace had picked up and, like their first epic battle, this fight was becoming another classic. Ali took the early lead, and Frazier came on to dominate the middle rounds, and Ali would swing right back and turn the momentum his way. Ali hurt Frazier once again in the 8th round, hitting him with tremendous shots that had Joe in trouble. But Frazier held his own in the 9th and 10th. This back and forth trend continued into the 11th and 12th rounds until both men seemed drained and had to call on all of their reserves to continue.

In the following rounds, though, Muhammad Ali's great pride and determination began to prevail, and he started to dominate Frazier completely. Then, in round 13, Ali blasted Frazier with a series of lefts and rights. He knocked Frazier's mouthpiece out of his mouth. And he really staggered Frazier and made him reel backwards. It was a tremendous round for Ali and was the beginning of the end for Joe Frazier. In the 14th round, Frazier's left eye was badly swollen and almost shut and he could not longer see Muhammad Ali's rights coming at him. Ali was now taking potshots at Frazier and Joe was being hit almost at will, being visibly hurt by the end of the round. If there had been another minute or so left, it is doubtful that Frazier would have lasted the 14th round. He was that close to being knocked out. However, the bell rang and Frazier was guided back to his corner by the referee.

Joe Frazier's trainer, Eddie Futch, looked his man over in the corner and determined that he had taken enough of a battering. Not willing to risk further injury to his fighter, Futch told the referee that it was over, and that Frazier would not continue. Muhammad Ali, slumped on the stool in his corner and visibly exhausted, had won "The Thriller in Manila", the rubber match of a three-fight series with Frazier in a grueling, hard-fought battle of two men who both had hearts of a champion.

Ali would later state that, *"Joe Frazier quit just before I did."* By this he meant that he may have considered not coming out for the 15th round due to exhaustion (though I have my doubts that Ali would have quit -- it just didn't seem to be in his nature). He would also claim that this fight *"...was the closest thing to death that I could feel."* After all the negative things that Ali had said about Joe Frazier, he said after this fight that, *"He is great! I don't know of any other fighter in the world, besides me, who could have beat Frazier the way he fought tonight."* And Frazier said of Ali, *"Man, I hit him with punches that'd bring down the walls of a city,"* then added, *"Lawdy, Lawdy, he's a great champion."*

This had been a war. The pace of the fight. The challenge, for Frazier, of trying to win back the title. The pressure, for Ali, of trying to keep the title. The accumulated effect of all the punches taken by both fighters. The amount of damage to brain and kidney tissue from such a brutal slugfest. And the tremendous heat and humidity of that evening. All of this took every ounce of courage, will and determination that both men could muster and most experts have questioned how much of these qualities were left in them when it was all through. Neither fighter would ever again fight at that same level. Frazier would never contend for the title again. Ali would go on, but would never be as punishing and dominant as he had been in fights of the past. The Thriller in Manila brought out the best in both Muhammad Ali and Joe Frazier, but it also brought them to the pinnacle of their respective careers.

Part 19 THE DECLINE

After the Joe Frazier fight, Ali would take on Jean Pierre Coopman in February 1976 and would defeat him with a fifth-round KO, but some of the difficulties Ali would come to have later began to show themselves. He was still the champ, however, time was beginning to take its toll. The first major signs of Ali's decline came when he fought Jimmy Young on April 30, 1976. Young was a talented fighter but was relatively inexperienced in general and especially when compared to Muhammad Ali, in particular. But he was a good defensive fighter and gave Ali lots of trouble. Ali's fight with Jimmy Young was very, very close and some thought that he may have even lost the fight. Ali got the decision in the end, but he might not have gotten it if Jimmy Young had not made the technical mistake of ducking his head through the ropes as a defensive strategy. This tactic cost Young some points in the eyes of the judges, and so Ali narrowly escaped with a victory. Ali would later KO Richard Dunn in round 5 in Munich, Germany. This KO by Muhammad Ali would be the last knockout of his career, another sign of the decline in his skills.

Part 20 ALI vs. NORTON III

But the real indicator that Muhammad Ali's career as a fighter was very much nearing its end was his third fight with Ken Norton in New York's Yankee Stadium, September 28, 1976. As in the previous two fights with Norton, the crab-like, 'peek-a-boo' style which Norton used gave Ali a lot of trouble. But now, Norton was in top form, more experienced and stronger than before, while Ali was on the decline due to natural aging. This fight was a very difficult one for Muhammad Ali but, still, his greatness as a boxer aided him enough to win a good number of rounds by outboxing and outscoring Norton and beating him to the punch.

As the 15th and final round began, the fight was so close that many felt that whoever won the 15th round would win the fight. But Ken Norton's corner made a very bad mistake. They assumed that Norton was well ahead on points, so they told him to fight the 15th round cautiously so as to avoid getting careless and lose by a knockout. As a result, Ali danced and jabbed Norton and avoided his attacks for most of the round, winning the round in the judges' eyes. It was this 15th round which then gave Ali the decision, and he had retained his title.

Norton and his cornermen were shocked and angry because they thought Norton had won enough rounds to get the decision. But Ali was given a unanimous decision. Sadly, however, when interviewed after the fight, Ali said that he, himself, felt he had lost that fight. He also later told his fight doctor, Dr. Ferdie Pacheco, that it was now time to stop and get out of boxing. Unfortunately, Ali did not follow his own good thinking, and he still continued on in boxing.

After the Norton fight, Ali would take on Alfredo Evangelista, a fighter who was not known for great boxing skills, and Ali would only win by a 15-round decision. He would then take on hard-hitting Earnie Shavers and would find himself involved in a war, because Shavers hit Ali at times with shots that must have done real damage to a now aging Muhammad Ali. Ali would win, again on a 15-round decision, but this fight must have taken a tremendous toll on him.

Part 21 THE LOSS OF THE TITLE

Muhammad Ali now decided to have an easy fight. He had been through a few wars with quite experienced fighters. Now it was time for an easy payday. He signed to fight a boxer who only had 6 professional fights. Ali was a veteran of 57 fights, having won 55 and only losing 2. What could possibly go wrong in a challenge from such an inexperienced youngster?

This young boxer had won the Olympic Gold Medal but, still, he was fighting someone considered by many as the greatest of all time. Ali did not train well, as he did not take this fight seriously at all. His weight ballooned up to around 230 before he started training, and then he only sparred 50 rounds in preparation for the fight. This young, inexperienced boxer was Leon Spinks, and Spinks would give Ali a lesson for all times -- never take too much for granted.

The two met on February 15, 1978, in Las Vegas, Nevada. Ali thought that in this fight he could wear down Spinks with the Rope-a-Dope, as he had done to Foreman. But being so young, Spinks never really tired. Ali did tire, however, and Spinks took full advantage. A fight that Ali thought would be a mere tune-up turned out to be a great upset. Ali fought back gallantly towards the end of the fight, but it was too little, too late. One of the judges scored 143-142, giving the fight to Ali. Another one scored 145-140, giving the fight to Spinks. But the deciding vote was 144-141 for the winner and NEW Heavyweight Champion of the World, Leon Spinks. His corner celebrated wildly. Unknown Leon Spinks had defeated the great Muhammad Ali and, for the first time in his career, Ali had lost his title in the ring. His work ethic had worked against him and now his title was gone. It belonged to Spinks. Muhammad Ali had suffered the 3rd defeat of his illustrious career.

Part 22 THREE-TIME CHAMPION

It now seemed, given his age, that it was finally time for Muhammad Ali to retire. After all, what was Ali to do -- try to win the title a third time? None of the great heavyweights of the past had accomplished such a feat. It was never done in the history of Heavyweight boxing. But this was the great Muhammad Ali. He did not want to follow history. He wanted to re-write it. So, despite the objections of the World Boxing Council (WBC) who wanted Spinks to fight Ken Norton (and the WBC would strip Spinks of their version of the title and give it to Norton), Muhammad Ali signed to fight Leon Spinks in a rematch, challenging him for what he had owned and lost - - the title of Heavyweight Champion of the World.

This rematch would take place on September 15, 1978 in New Orleans, Louisiana and, this time, Ali had trained correctly with the opportunity of regaining the title staring him in the face. This time Ali would dance and stick, using the style which had made him a lifetime winner and the greatest fighter of all time. He floated. He stung. He dominated Spinks from start to finish. When it was all over, one judge scored the fight 10 rounds-Ali, 4 rounds-Spinks, with 1 even. The second judge scored it 11 rounds-Ali, 4 rounds-Spinks. The third judge scored it 10 rounds-Ali, 4 rounds-Spinks, with 1 even, and history had been made. Muhammad Ali had become the first Heavyweight boxer in history to win the title three times. Ali had won back his title. He was, once again, the NEW Heavyweight Champion of the World. He had defeated Spinks convincingly to avenge the third loss of his career. He had climbed back to the top. This was the second historic moment that Muhammad Ali had to fulfill. But this would not be a new beginning for the great Muhammad Ali. It was the end. Muhammad Ali would never win another fight after this historic evening. In June 1979, Ali announced his retirement from the ring. He went out on top, 56 wins against 3 losses, and retired as the Heavyweight Champion of the World. And he was now widely recognized by most as the greatest fighter of all time.

Part 23 COMEBACKS AND RETIREMENT

It is with great regret that Muhammad Ali did not allow his historic and triumphant title victory over Leon Spinks to be the end of his boxing story. Rather, two years after his retirement Muhammad Ali would decide, because of a number of unfortunate pressures upon him, to attempt a comeback and try to win the title, for the 4th time, from the then-reigning Champion, Larry Holmes. For Muhammad Ali, retirement was not an easy way of life. He missed the limelight. He missed the competition. However, he didn't necessarily miss the hard training. In the two years that he had been out of boxing, Ali had naturally gained some weight and now he had to try and go back to training to bring his weight down and get into shape. He wanted to speed up the process, and what happened next could have cost him his life.

Ali went to see a doctor who, mistakenly, determined that Ali was suffering from a hyperthyroid condition. As a result of this misdiagnosis, Ali was given medication which helped him to lose 30 pounds in a short period of time. Angelo Dundee said that Ali looked like his old self, but this medication also created some medical problems for Ali, coupled with the fact that Ali was now suffering from the early effects of Parkinson's, although this was not fully known as of yet.

The negative effects of all this became evident on the night of the fight with Holmes. On the evening of October 2, 1980, Ali made his attempted comeback against Heavyweight Champion Larry Holmes and, in Round 1, Ali seemed to be simply checking out Holmes and not doing anything offensively in the fight. Yet, by the end of the first round, Ali was already tiring. Something was definitely wrong.

In the proceeding rounds, Ali seemed to be either unwilling or unable to throw any punches and simply tried fending off Holmes' offenses. This was not the Muhammad Ali that the world had known in the past. Soon, Ali was simply being battered by Holmes and could not retaliate. He tried to dance in Round 7 and actually did well enough to win that round. But something was still quite wrong with Ali. He was not sweating, an effect from the medication he should never have been taking. It was all downhill, as Holmes teed off on Ali time and time again. After round 11, Angelo Dundee had seen enough. He was not going to risk any damage to this boxing legend. He stopped the fight. Ali's attempted comeback had failed.

Ali went to the hospital on one of the days following the fight because he knew that he had not been himself during that Holmes' fight. But Parkinson's would still not be diagnosed yet. We would only learn a few years later that Parkinson's Syndrome had also played a role, along with the medication, in what was wrong with Ali that night.

Once again, for Muhammad Ali, retirement just did not seem to be in his vocabulary. He did not want to go out sitting on his stool with a TKO loss, the only time in his career that he would ever be stopped. He wanted to put on a better showing, for at least one "Last Hurrah". Muhammad Ali would make his final comeback a year later, on December 11, 1981, noticeably different than he was in the Holmes' fight, exhibiting much slower reflexes, and would lose a 10-round decision to Trevor Berbick, although his performance would be better this night than it was against Larry Holmes. However, after this failed comeback against Berbick, Muhammad Ali, himself, now knew for sure that time had caught up with him. He knew now that he could no longer float like a butterfly, nor sting like a bee, nor do what it took to fight competitively in professional boxing. Age and health had now stopped him. After the Berbick fight, Muhammad Ali announced his retirement from boxing for the final time, and he would never box professionally again.

It had been a long and successful road for Muhammad Ali, spanning 21 years as a pro, 61 professional fights, winning 56 and losing 5. Two of the five losses took place after he had initially retired, so in his regular professional career, Ali had only suffered three losses - - to Joe Frazier, Ken Norton, and Leon Spinks - - and would turn around and defeat Frazier and Norton twice each, and defeat Spinks once, all to avenge those three losses. He defeated Sonny Liston against all the odds. He defeated George Foreman against all the odds. He won the title three times, and was the first Heavyweight ever to do so.

Of all the fighters in boxing history, Muhammad Ali stands out in speed of hand, speed of foot, in beating the odds, and in world popularity. Of all the fighters in boxing history, indeed, Muhammad Ali stands out as the Greatest of All Time.

Muhammad Ali's List of Fights
56 Wins – 5 Losses – 37 KO's

1960

October 29 - Tunney Hunsaker, Louisville, KY - W 6

December 27 - Herb Siler, Miami Beach, FL - KO 4

1961

January 17 - Tony Esperti, Miami Beach, FL - KO 3

February 7 - Jim Robinson, Miami Beach, FL - KO 1

February 21 - Donnie Fleeman, Miami Beach, FL - KO 7

April 19 - Lamar Clark, Louisville, KY - KO 2

June 26 - Duke Sabedong, Las Vegas, NV - W 10

July 22 - Alonzo Johnson, Louisville, KY - W 10

October 7 - Alex Miteff, Louisville, KY - KO 6

November 29 - Willi Besmanoff, Louisville, KY - KO 7

1962

February 19 - Sonny Banks, New York, NY - KO 4

March 28 - Don Warner, Miami Beach, FL - KO 4

April 23 - George Logan, Los Angeles, CA - KO 6

May 19 - Billy Daniels, New York, NY - KO 7

July 20 - Alejandro Lavorante, Los Angeles, CA - KO 5

November 15 - Archie Moore, Los Angeles, CA - KO 4

1963

January 24 - Charlie Powell, Pittsburgh, PA - KO 3

March 13 - Doug Jones, New York, NY - W 10

June 18 - Henry Cooper, London - KO 5

1964

February 25 - Sonny Liston, Miami Beach, FL - KO 7

Muhammad Ali wins the Heavyweight Title

1965

May 25 - Sonny Liston, Lewiston, ME - KO 1

November 22 - Floyd Patterson, Las Vegas, NV - KO 12

1966

March 29 - George Chuvalo, Toronto - W 15

May 21 - Henry Cooper, London - KO 6

August 6 - Brian London, London - KO 3

September 10 - Karl Mildenberger, Frankfurt,Germany - KO 12

November 14 - Cleveland Williams, Houston, TX - KO 3

1967

February 6 - Ernie Terrell, Houston, TX - W 15
March 22 - Zora Folley, New York, NY - KO 7
Ali is stripped of his title in April, for refusing the military draft on religious grounds.

1970

Ali returns to boxing after three-and-a-half year layoff.

October 26 - Jerry Quarry, Atlanta, GA - KO 3

December 7 - Oscar Bonavena, New York, NY - KO 15

1971
March 8 - Joe Frazier, New York, NY - L 15
Ali loses Heavyweight Title match.
It is his 1st loss as a Professional.
Frazier is now the Undisputed Heavyweight Champion.

July 26 - Jimmy Ellis, Houston, TX - KO 12

November 17 - Buster Mathis, Houston, TX - W 12

December 26 - Jurgen Blin, Zurich, Switzerland - KO 7

1972

April 1 - Mac Foster, Tokyo, Japan - W 15

May 1 - George Chuvalo, Vancouver, Canada - W 12

June 29 - Jerry Quarry, Las Vegas, NV - KO 7

July 19 - Al 'Blue' Lewis, Dublin - KO 11

September 20 - Floyd Patterson, New York, NY - KO 7

November 21 - Bob Foster, Stateline, NV - KO 8

1973

February 14 - Joe Bugner, Las Vegas, NV - W 12
March 31 - Ken Norton, San Diego, CA - L 12
**Jaw is broken in 2nd round, but Ali fights 10 more rounds.
Loses by decision.   Only the 2nd loss of Ali's career.**

September 10 - Ken Norton, Los Angeles, CA - W 12

October 20 - Rudi Lubbers, Jakarta, Indonesia - W 12

1974

January 28 - Joe Frazier, New York, NY - W 12
October 30 - George Foreman, Kinshasa, Zaire - KO 8
**Muhammad Ali Regains the Heavyweight Title,
becoming only the 2nd Heavyweight to ever do so.**

1975

March 24 - Chuck Wepner, Cleveland, OH - KO 15

May 16 - Ron Lyle, Las Vegas, NV - KO 11

June 30 - Joe Bugner, Kuala Lumpur, Malaysia - W 15

October 1 - Joe Frazier, Manila, Philippines - KO 14

1976

February 20 - Jean Pierre Coopman, San Juan, PR - KO 5

April 30 - Jimmy Young, Landover, MD - W 15

May 24 - Richard Dunn, Munich, Germany - KO 5

September 28 - Ken Norton, New York, NY - W 15

1977

May 16 - Alfredo Evangelista, Landover, MD - W 15

September 29 - Earnie Shavers, New York, NY - W 15

1978
February 15 - Leon Spinks, Las Vegas, NV - L 15
**Ali loses the Heavyweight Title by Split-Decision.
It is the 3rd Loss of Ali's Career.**

September 15 - Leon Spinks, New Orleans, LA - W 15
**Muhammad Ali wins the Heavyweight Title for the 3rd time,
becoming the first Heavyweight in boxing history to do so.**

Muhammad Ali announces his retirement from boxing.

1980
October 2 - Larry Holmes, Las Vegas, NV - L by TKO 11
**Ali makes a failed comeback after 2-year layoff and loses
in an attempt to win Title for the 4th time.**

1981

December 11 - Trevor Berbick, Nassau, Bahamas - L 10

Ali loses again in a final failed comeback attempt.

MUHAMMAD ALI retires from boxing for good.

FILMS BY OR ABOUT MUHAMMAD ALI:

On this page, we list some of the more important films which were made either by Muhammad Ali or about him, showcasing his skills and personality inside and outside of the ring. This list is not all-inclusive, and does not cover the many appearances by Muhammad Ali on various talk shows, documentaries, and sports programs, as well as cameo appearances on numerous TV shows. It is merely a brief listing of movies, video cassettes and DVDs which have been and still are available to the public about this great champion, Muhammad Ali.

ALI - (2001)
Starring Will Smith as Muhammad Ali, depicting the life and career of Ali.

MUHAMMAD ALI: Through the Eyes of the World - (2001)
An account of the life of Muhammad Ali, told by family, friends and fans from all over the world.

MUHAMMAD ALI: IN HIS OWN WORDS - (1998)
A documentary showing Muhammad Ali as a public speaker, as well as a boxing icon.

WHEN WE WERE KINGS - (1996)
Documentary which covers the events surrounding the "Rumble in the Jungle" with George Foreman.

MUHAMMAD ALI: THE WHOLE STORY - (1996)
Originally a six-episode TV mini-series, this DVD set is a 5-hour marathon of events in the life of Muhammad Ali.

THE GREATEST, POUND FOR POUND - (1994)
A documentary which discusses the question, 'Who was the best fighter of all time?" Boxing historians Bill Cayton and Bert Randolph Sugar look at several greats of the past, including Muhammad Ali, Sugar Ray Robinson, Rocky Marciano, Joe Louis, and Henry Armstrong.

CHAMPIONS FOREVER - (1989)
A boxing documentary with commentary by and about several great champions: Muhammad Ali, George Foreman, Larry Holmes, Joe Frazier, Ken Norton and Mike Tyson.

FREEDOM ROAD - (1979)
Muhammad Ali as 'Gideon Jackson', an ex-slave who became a Senator, but still had to wage many battles against racism.

THE GREATEST - (1977)
Muhammad Ali as himself, based on his autobiography, "The Greatest: My Own Story"

MUHAMMAD ALI: SKILL, BRAINS AND GUTS - (1975)
A look at the boxing career of Muhammad Ali.   87 minutes

ALI THE MAN, ALI THE FIGHTER - (1971)
Documentary which highlights Ali's battles outside the ring as well as in boxing.

A.K.A. CASSIUS CLAY - (1970)
An early documentary about Muhammad Ali, 'also known as' Cassius Clay.

MUHAMMAD ALI

IN ISLAM

Muhammad Ali performing prayer
Photo by Walter Iooss, Jr. - Sports Illustrated

One reason why some people had problems with Muhammad Ali was because of his religious beliefs. I have written this page, called "Muhammad Ali in Islam", in an attempt to explain and clarify some of the problems with Ali's beliefs (of that time period) from the point of view of the social circumstances, from the misunderstandings of people, in general, and from what Ali, himself, did not know at the time was incorrect in his beliefs. I begin this section on Muhammad

Ali in Islam from the most important aspect of his belief -- the concept of God.

In the early 1960's, Muhammad Ali belonged to a group called the Nation of Islam. He was introduced to this organization, either directly or indirectly, through Malcolm X, and both men gave their allegiance to the leader of the Nation of Islam, Elijah Muhammad. Elijah claimed to have been taught by someone named Wallace Fard Muhammad, whom Elijah referred to as "Master Fard". Herein lies the first and most critical problem with Muhammad Ali's beliefs at that time (circa 1962-1963). Elijah believed that God, whom the Muslim world correctly refers to as Allah, came to Earth in the person of Master Fard Muhammad. This was an immeasurable mistake because, in Islam, there is no such belief as God manifesting Himself in any person, nor in any thing. Not only is it foreign to Islam, but it is the very opposite of the concept of God in Islam.

The second major mistake was the totally erroneous belief that Elijah Muhammad was the Messenger of Allah (God). Again, Islam is very clear in its system of belief that Prophet Muhammad of Arabia, who lived more than 1400 years ago, was the Messenger of Allah (God) and the last of the Prophets.

So this was another critical error with Muhammad Ali's beliefs in Islam at that time.

A third problem with the belief system of Muhammad Ali in Islam, at that time, pertained to some of the general teachings of Elijah Muhammad. In the Nation of Islam, as it was called, Elijah Muhammad taught that black people were gods and white people were devils. It quickly becomes instantly clear, then, why some people would have a problem with Muhammad Ali. While this ideology was very wrong and, again, foreign to Islam, we must, however, take a look at the circumstances which contributed to some people believing in such a false concept, despite how strangely it sounded.

It is quite true that many white people were not exactly treating black people as their equals, to say the least. Racism was rampant in the United States with the Ku Klux Klan, a white supremist group, along with others, terrorizing, torturing, and murdering black people at will. How often were black people found hanging from trees, or burnt at a stake, or cut in half on railroad tracks, all at the hands of some racist white people? Did not Muhammad Ali see and hear these reports quite often? Look at the differences in those days in educational quality, job opportunities and economic and housing standards between white and black, primarily as a result of racism. Were these effects of racism not evident in Muhammad Ali's time? Was not America's portrayal of blacks through its white-owned media quite negative?

The times were racially charged. Some of Elijah's teachings, when they were delivered by such an eloquent and gifted speaker as Malcolm X was, could often be made to almost sound believable during a time of violence, segregation, and Jim Crow laws, especially when Elijah's erroneous ideology was followed up by true and accurate accounts of white brutality against black people. Muhammad Ali was trapped in that time frame. He was not as much the promoter of the ideology as he was a victim of the circumstances and the times. Some disliked him because of his beliefs, but some hated him, also, simply because he was black. So while those teachings contained many false ideas about gods and devils, and heaven and hell being right here on Earth, not everything which came out of the mouth of Muhammad Ali was false.

A racist is always an enemy to the idea of man living in harmony with other races. In that light, Muhammad Ali saw *'white' America* (but not every individual white person) as his enemy. He always had some whites around him, some being very close to him, like Gene Kilroy, artist LeRoy Neiman, and most especially, he had Angelo Dundee, his trusted trainer and confidant. Conversely, he saw non-whites as his brothers and sisters, who shared his suffering with him from an oppressive enemy. Included in that brotherhood were the Vietnamese people. He saw them as victims of America's racism and arrogance. It is in this light that we should then try to understand why Muhammad Ali said, when told that he was going to be drafted, *"I ain't got no quarrel with them Vietcong."* He also said, *"No Vietcong ever called me 'Nigger'."* In view of the social circumstances of that time, this profound statement made perfectly good sense. The U.S. government was telling Ali to take part in a war where those whom he saw as his opposers were sending him to kill those who were not his opposers.

Look at what Ali, himself, had to say in reference to this draft:

"Why should they ask me to put on a uniform and go 10,000 miles from home and drop bombs and bullets on Brown people in Vietnam while so-called Negro people in Louisville are treated like dogs and denied simple human rights? No, I'm not going 10,000 miles from home to help murder and burn another poor nation simply to continue the domination of white slave masters of the darker people the world over. This is the day when such evils must come to an end. I have been

warned that to take such a stand would cost me millions of dollars. But I have said it once and I will say it again. The real enemy of my people is here. I will not disgrace my religion, my people or myself by becoming a tool to enslave those who are fighting for their own justice, freedom and equality. If I thought the war was going to bring freedom and equality to 22 million of my people they wouldn't have to draft me, I'd join tomorrow. I have nothing to lose by standing up for my beliefs. So I'll go to jail, so what? We've been in jail for 400 years."

So, it turned out that Muhammad Ali became disliked for being black, for his religious beliefs, and for his position on the draft. This section of the book, however, is called "Muhammad Ali in Islam", so I will finish by focusing on that theme.

It is necessary, in order to be fair, to point out that while some of Muhammad Ali's prior beliefs, which offended people, were not the correct beliefs in Islam, many in the United States were vehemently opposed to even the most correct teachings and practices of Islam. That was true then, and it is still very true even to this day. And Muhammad Ali cannot be blamed for that. The people for whom this holds true must be blamed. Prejudice is the fault of no one except the one who does the pre-judging, especially without knowledge of that which they judge.

To correctly see Muhammad Ali in relation to the religion of Islam is to first see where he was, and why his beliefs were as they were at that time, and take note of the many incorrect parts. Secondly, one must see how Muhammad Ali's belief in Islam evolved from belief in a "man-god" (and we seek refuge from such belief) and from belief in a self-proclaimed messenger, into one who came to understand that the basic foundation of his religion, Islam, is that "Nothing deserves to be worshipped except Allah (the Creator), alone, who has no partners, and that Prophet Muhammad (born in 570, died in 632) is the last Messenger of Allah."

In 1975, Elijah Muhammad died, and with him died the incorrect beliefs which had been ascribed to both he and Fard Muhammad. Muhammad Ali learned that his past beliefs had numerous false elements, mixed in with some very good socially uplifting elements, so he dropped the false parts, kept the good, and moved into more mainstream, orthodox Islam. No longer can he be blamed for harboring anti-white rhetoric or racially inflammatory teachings. Those days are long gone and Muhammad Ali in Islam has a new meaning. It is belief in the Oneness of God, in His Angels, in His Books, in His Messengers (all of them), in the Day of Judgment, and in the Ultimate Will of God. That is true Islam. And it is in this light and this light, alone, that we must now view Muhammad Ali in Islam.

EPILOGUE

MUHAMMAD ALI TODAY

Now, the poetic voice of Muhammad Ali is silent. The limbs of his body shake from his battles with Parkinson's Disease, a neurological disorder that he has been hampered with for the last 20 or so years. These days, however, he still makes several public appearances, and he still loves the attention that he receives when he walks into a room and all in attendance stop – and look – and simply admire the presence of "The Greatest" in their midst. He has not lost his public appeal. He has not lost his love of the public that adores him. He has not lost his playfulness, for you will occasionally see him pose for photographers and throw a jab at the air, as he had thrown at so many an opponent in younger, faster, smoother days. All he has lost is the fluidity of motion that Parkinson's Disease steals from its victims. And the speech is not as it was, so Ali remains silent.

He has said, as have those who are close to him like his loyal wife, Lonnie, that you should not feel sorry for him as he has no regrets about his life. If he had to do it all over again, he would do what he did before – box, like so few had done before him or after him – and stand up for his beliefs, like so few had the courage to do, so bravely and boldly, before his time and since then.

He is still Muhammad Ali, and what you should do when you see him, or read about him, or think about him, or see a documentary about him, is simply admire him, respect him for the sacrifices he has made, thank him for the encouragement he has given to so many others, and be grateful for him – for he has been an inspiration to sports fans and non-sports fans, the young and the old, the well-off and the poor, those who are healthy as well as those who are sick – and say a prayer for him that God makes this difficult, trying illness as easy for him as it can be. And be happy for him – for he accomplished so much that many of us will never be capable of accomplishing – and take your hat off to him – for most of us would never had been able to handle the fame that he had, for he was and possibly still is, the most famous person on the planet Earth.

But if you are a fan of the sport of boxing, then all you can do is look up to him – for no one transformed that sport, or any other sport, like Muhammad Ali did. No matter what his critics, his detractors and his depreciators have to say about him, boxing has never seen the likes of a Muhammad Ali –

except for those few glorious years when he graced the boxing ring with his presence – and we, who were blessed with the opportunity to see him, should all be thankful that we did.

Boxing is not the same anymore. Instead of having a great champion like Ali at the top, we have a whole heap of champions that rotate like a game of musical chairs from one month to the next. It has never been the same – nay, sports has never been the same – since Muhammad Ali left the ring, so let us appreciate the greatness that he gave the sport of boxing and the world of athletics. Let us appreciate the legacy that he has left us with as a man who stood up for his principles, and defied the odds – inside the ring and outside of the ring – and won. He was one of a kind. He was, in the world of boxing, the Greatest of All Time.

He was – and maybe, symbolically, he still is, and he just might always be – the Heavyweight Champion of the World, **Muhammad Ali.**

www.ingramcontent.com/pod-product-compliance
Lightning Source LLC
Chambersburg PA
CBHW022028090426
42739CB00006BA/340